Navigating the
Debt Relief Maze:

Chapter 7 Bankruptcy and
Chapter 13 Bankruptcy Explained

Alexzander C. J. Adams, Esq.

First Edition	September 2014
Second Edition	January 2015
Third Edition	June 2015
Fourth Edition	June 2018
Editor & Book Design	Jana Seitzer, GeekGirlDigital.com
Printing	CreateSpace

ISBN: 978-0-692-28868-9

This book covers only United States bankruptcy law. This text is not a substitute for personalized legal advice from a bankruptcy lawyer. Please consult an attorney for further information. Statement in compliance with 11 U.S.C. 528(a)(4) "We are a debt relief agency. We help people file for bankruptcy relief under the Bankruptcy Code."

Nothing in this book is designed to provide legal advice to the reader. This is written in a manner so a non-attorney may understand a little bit about how bankruptcy works. Should you desire to file bankruptcy or explore your options, I strongly encourage you to schedule a time to meet with an attorney to discuss your options. We are available at (844)-BK-DEBTS or via email at newclient@PortlandBK.com. If you are in Oregon or Washington, I am happy to provide a free consultation regarding bankruptcy if it is an option you are considering. I handle bankruptcy cases state wide in Oregon and Washington depending on my case load. Thank you for reading this book.

Praise for Law Offices of
Alexzander C. J. Adams, P.C.

"Alexzander Adams is an excellent truly caring Lawyer. I came to Alexz with a pile of worries. He separated me from the dark place I was in and helped me back to financial stability. Yes, there was doubt, but only mine! He always had faith I would get through it. Yes, it was a long recovery, 3 years, but [i]n November [ ], he informed me my ordeal was over. He's the lawyer you want, but really it's up to you! Trust your future to Alexzander. You'll be happy with your decision."

"Alexz and his staff were supportive and professional during a very difficult time for me. They made the scary process of filing for bankruptcy not only understandable, but they were also personable, supportive and compassionate. And the results were so much more positive than I could ever have imagined!

I researched 25 lawyers, and interviewed four before I chose Alexz. With each Lawyer I spoke with, I told them I was interviewing others, and they all asked me who else I was talking to. Each of them had heard of Alexz, but had never heard of any of the others, and all of them said that I would be in excellent hands if I hired Alexz. I had not wanted to drive to Beaverton from Portland, but when I met with Alexz, and he answered all of my questions patiently and thoroughly and provided additional information, I hired him on the spot.

I highly recommend Alexz, without reservation, and am so glad I found him and his firm. They turned a scary and difficult time of my life into a positive and rewarding experience. He is competent, intelligent, and caring. You will not go wrong choosing Alexz."

"Found ourselves in the predicament of a lifetime, thinking this was the end of the road for our house, life, and financial hardship. [We hired] the Law offices of Alexzander C.J. Adams with no second thought. We found the confidence to continue with Mr. Adams in our Chapter 13 case and with tremendous satisfaction, we can now move on to our life, goals, and priorities. From [our] family, Thank you Mr. Adams!"

"My wife and I have been through a lot of struggles in the last 18 years. Neither of us knew that it would help to change our lives. Alexzander and his team have seriously been the greatest, very personal and positive thinking individuals. Thank you so much for all of your help."

About the Author

Mr. Adams is a practicing consumer bankruptcy and litigation lawyer in the Portland, Oregon area. He is a member of the Oregon and Washington States Bar Associations. Mr. Adams received his undergraduate degrees in Marketing and Economics from Towson University in Maryland, where he also minored in guitar performance. He went on to receive a Master's in Business Administration from the University of Baltimore, where he also focused on marketing and finance. He received his law degree from Western State University in Fullerton, California. While in law school, he was on the editorial board of the Law Review being voted Outstanding Editorial Board Member, maintained a full academic scholarship for the duration of his studies, externed with the Orange County District Attorney's Offices, and somehow found time to clerk for the Honorable Richard T. Fields, then presiding judge of Riverside Superior Court in Riverside California.

Intro

This little book is now coming into the 5th printing. Since the first edition of this book, there has been incredible turmoil in the financial industry and our political process has suffered tremendous polarization from both sides. It seems like the banks and institutions we trusted with our money and our mortgages have failed us as a society. Many have been caught red handed lying, cheating, stealing, and manipulating reality in a way which doesn't serve their customers and clients, nor the citizenry or our country, that grants these institutions the right to engage in business here. And then there's the political turmoil. Perhaps there has been no greater time in our nation's history that the odds are steeped so sharply against the working and middle classes.

But bankruptcy, should it match your needs, is a powerful equalizer for the millions that file each year. Most debts can be eliminated, garnishments are stopped, collections call go away, and life gets back to normal. For others who take advantage of chapter 13's provision, delinquent taxes can be paid, past due child support can be caught up, foreclosures are on hold, and outrageous car loan interest rates can be brought back to a normal level among other things. I call this the shield of bankruptcy - shielding you from oppressive, life crushing debt and providing a fast path back on track for most of my client.

But what happens, like above, when you follow the rules and your creditors don't? There is a whole additional level of protection in bankruptcy I call the sword. Like President Roosevelt said, to speak softly and carry a big stick in bankruptcy means that if your creditors follow the rules, everything will go as planned. But if they don't, the bankruptcy system itself carries a very powerful stick (or sword as I refer to it) to use in the enforcement of your rights.

What does this look like?

1. What if you file a bankruptcy; but a creditor continues to collect against you (in violation of the bankruptcy stay order or discharge injunction order)?
2. What if a creditor refuses to return property to you that you are entitled to after you file bankruptcy?
3. What happens if a creditor attempts to foreclosure upon you even though you are under the court's protection?
4. What happens when a creditor disobeys a court order and costs you time and money to fight their illegal action?

There are lots of other scenarios, but you get the idea. Sadly, there are times that the above, and in some cases, even more outrageous behavior, occurs to your by your creditors.

The bankruptcy court is a court; just like you would imagine a court would be. It routinely hears claims and lawsuits involved in the bankruptcy process. And, in fact, when creditors do not follow the rules, one possibility is to sue the creditor in bankruptcy court for violating the rules. This is a very powerful solution to stop the creditor from ongoing harassment.

My office routinely pursues illegal activities perpetrated by creditors in bankruptcy. Most times, they are required to STOP the egregious behavior, PAY my clients for the harassment (this is called damages), and PAY for all of the extra attorney fees required to prosecute the claim. There is typically no cost to my clients for this extra level of service as the creditors have to pay the legal fees associated with this, and in fact, on many occasions, my clients have paid their legal fees for the bankruptcy, and a few months later I present my clients for the money my office recovered from the creditors for their egregious and often outrageous behavior.

Think about what I wrote. On many occasions over the past years, I've paid my clients more in damages than they initially paid me to do the bankruptcy. This means I PAY THEM TO GET THEM OUT OF DEBT.

Of course, this doesn't happen in every case, but it happens in enough cases for me to update this book to notify you that this is a possibly in every bankruptcy I take on. I've included an appendix to this book called "Bankruptcy Violations and how to report them to your attorney." Should you decided to hire a different bankruptcy attorney, make sure part of their representation includes pursuing what I call these Rogue Creditors when it is needed.

Be sure to read this chapter. There will be an update to my website with more information as well, but this sets the stage for the new debt free life you are embarking on.

Congratulations on having the courage to pursue life debt free. I look forward to assisting you should you decide to pursue bankruptcy.

Contents

About the Author.. v

Intro vii

1 Who Am I?... 1

2 What If I Can't Afford to Hire an Attorney and File
   Bankruptcy...3

3 Will You Lose Your Home or Other Stuff in Bankruptcy?..9

4 Does Bankruptcy Stop a Garnishment or Lawsuit
   Against My Pay?..13

5 What About My Retirement Account?........................... 17

6 Will I Ever Be Able to Get Credit Again?...................... 21

7 Why Do People End Up Filing Bankruptcy?................. 25

8 What's the Difference Between Chapter 7 Bankruptcy
   and Chapter 13 Bankruptcy?....................................... 27

9 Do You Have to Pay Back All Your Debt in Chapter 13
   Bankruptcy?... 31

10 Who Are You?.. 35

11 Is It True That Bankruptcy Represents a Personal or
    Even a Moral Failure? 39

12 When Can I File The Case? 47

13 Can Bankruptcy Help With Tax Debt? 51

    Conclusion.. 53

    Closing Thoughts... 55

    Appendix.. 57

1. Who Am I?

Every day I get up and work to protect people from all different walks of life from the oppression that can result from unpaid debts. I stop home foreclosures, I resolve tax obligations, I stop garnishments, I reinstate driver's licenses, I help people catch up on mortgage arrears, and I resolve many different types of other financial problems. But my firm has a purpose beyond simply making money. It is also my job to help my clients turn their ship around, cut the anchors of past overwhelming debts, and push them back out into sea of life. There are real benefits to my individual clients in the work I perform—work that is based on the fact that a lawyer is nothing other than a service professional. I strive to treat my clients as a plumber or an electrician might treat their clients—providing great service at a reasonable price when the work is needed.

I have heard hundreds of times over the years that I don't come across like other lawyers that my clients have known and that they appreciate the directness of my approach. I take great pride in this. I started my journey toward being a lawyer early after I ended up in court over some trouble in high school. I was lucky in that I had a skilled trial lawyer defend me against the accusations that had been made against me. The power this lawyer was able to wield against my opponents to defend me and prove my case was amazing. I'd never seen anything like it. The words the lawyer used had stronger hits than any punch I had ever imagined might have against my opponents. I thought that it would be an awesome thing to do if I could help those in need in the same way—and it would be even better if it was a job—and better still if it paid money! So after chasing my dream of playing guitar and bass by touring with a band, I went to law school to become a trial lawyer. After law school, I discovered that same passion for the fight exists in protecting my clients from the results of unmanageable debts and helping clients work through their personal financial issues through consumer bankruptcy cases. In bankruptcy, I get to stop—usually dead in their tracks—the relentless creditor harassment of my clients. I am also able to quickly and efficiently relieve most, if not all, of the financial problems and debt burdens my clients carry with them. And once that happens to a person, some amazing things occur, things that I'm incredibly lucky to see on a daily basis in my practice. For example:

- Single parents working two jobs to pay off old debts can now work one job and spend time with their family;
- People who have been beaten into submission by ruthless creditor phone calls can now answer their phone with confidence that they will not be emotionally harassed;
- People with no focus and no drive because of crushing debt payments can now move on with their lives and build their dreams;
- Business people who have lost a business can focus on building new businesses;
- Stress from the crushing debt is replaced with optimism regarding the future.

The list goes on.

Often times, I say the first positive thing to my clients about their situation that they can remember hearing in a very long time. In my work, I get to provide hope, a better future, and a greatly improved quality of life to an amazing group of people. The tremendous positive difference that I'm able to make in my clients' lives is very powerful and I take it very seriously. This is who I am, and this is why I love being a consumer bankruptcy attorney.

2. What If I Can't Afford to Hire an Attorney and File Bankruptcy?

Having competent legal representation is critical whenever you go before a court. Make no mistake—this is United States Federal Bankruptcy Court. Literally, you must not make a mistake when you file your bankruptcy. And when you make a mistake, there are real world consequences. These include loss of assets, delays in process, failure to protect secured assets such as home and cars, failure to receive or revocation of your discharge—and in some cases—even criminal consequences.

Is it possible to fill out paperwork and file a bankruptcy without an attorney? Absolutely. The courts call people who file bankruptcy without an attorney "pro se" debtors. Is it worth it? No. Compared to other legal matters, hiring an attorney for bankruptcy is very cost effective considering the benefits and protection that you receive. Why is that? Well, let's take a look.

In bankruptcy, everything pretty much focuses on the day you file the bankruptcy—that is, the day that you swear under oath that everything is listed and accurate in your paperwork. This includes all debts, assets, income, transfers, household budget, and other personal and financial information. About a month after the case is filed, you will sit in front of a trustee and answer questions under oath about the information you provided regarding this day. Both the paperwork and your oral testimony must be consistent (as well as honest and candid).

What if you forgot to list some property on the bankruptcy paperwork? Well, the trustee can take the property. What if you failed to use an exemption to protect some property? A trustee can take that property. What if you didn't do this or that? There are real world consequences in bankruptcy that I see time and again that would have been easily avoided had the person simply chosen to be represented by an experienced bankruptcy attorney.

Let's look at just a few of these situations:

- Unreported transfers: Payments and transfers to creditors—especially to friends and family—are troublesome in bankruptcy. The court is concerned that you are paying or giving away things to friends and family instead of paying your creditors. To make the payments more "fair" to everyone, the trustee in a bankruptcy case has the power to void transfers and recover the items. Did you pay back your daughter $2,500 from your tax return and then file bankruptcy? Guess what? A trustee can demand that money back from your daughter. Did you recently gift a car or vehicle to someone? The trustee can recover that car, sell it, and pay something to your creditors. The court does not care that you believe the minivan, which you gave to a friend because they needed safe transportation for work or for their kids, should not be recovered.

- Missing information: Bankruptcy is all about disclosure. In exchange for relief from debt, you must be candid with the court and your creditors about your situation—what you have, what you don't have, what your income is, and—to a certain extent—what you ended up doing with things you did have in the past. If you do no tell the court something, it can affect your future for years to come. Are you involved in a motor vehicle lawsuit where you may recover significant money? If the claim against the other driver is not on your bankruptcy petition, the insurance company can say your claim doesn't exist IN THE OTHER LAWSUIT because you failed to disclose it in the bankruptcy! Fail to correctly list budget income and expenses, family members, or properly complete the means test? The court can compel you to provide this information and perhaps force you into Chapter 13 bankruptcy rather than a Chapter 7 bankruptcy.

- Incorrectly used exemptions: If you do not properly exempt the assets you do have, the court can theoretically TAKE ALL YOUR ASSETS. Although this doesn't usually happen, the court can cherry pick what it wants to liquidate if you have not properly protected what you do have or if you have failed to plan to protect what you have. This means the quad off-road cycle that you love to ride on the weekends is fair game for the court if it is not properly protected.

- Unreported assets: There are basically two ways that this becomes an issue. First, you forget or don't know that something should be listed. Perhaps you didn't think being on the title to a grandparent's house mattered; perhaps you are a joint bank account holder for your church; and perhaps you are holding assets for someone else. Although had you known—or perhaps a better word is understood—what was happening and how it really worked, these errors would not have been made and everything would have been properly disclosed to the court. Failure to list these assets can and does result in the forfeiture of the assets to the bankruptcy court. Sometimes this is something I can repair if I am hired after you have already filed a bankruptcy on your own— sometimes not. Second, if you intentionally misrepresented or failed to report required information, it can result in a forfeiture of your bankruptcy discharge and potential criminal charges.

- Chapter 13 in general: Chapter 13 is almost completely too nuanced and complicated to attempt without attorney representation. There are a lot of reasons for this, but central is the fact that in Chapter 13, you are generally in the driver's

seat, whereas in Chapter 7, once filed, you are sort of a
motivated participant following orders. About once per year
at weekly Chapter 13 confirmation hearings I attend, a pro
se debtor will show up and the trustee will announce that the
debtor got everything done and present an order confirming
the Chapter 13 plan to the court. The judge will congratulate
the debtor because it is extremely rare for a debtor to make
it that far (even though there are still 3–5 years more to go
in most cases). More typically, when a pro se debtor is on
the confirmation calendar, there is a stern warning from
the judge and trustee to find an attorney to handle the case
or face the risk of the case being dismissed, as there are
typically many things unresolved at this initial confirmation.
I have seen a judge tell the poor debtor to turn around, look
at the room full of attorneys behind them, and to talk to
one of them or their case will almost surely fail. I can only
imagine how scary that situation must be for the debtor
trying to navigate the waters of bankruptcy alone!

The risks and costs to filing a bankruptcy without an attorney are
significant. You don't go to a doctor, get a diagnosis, and then go
out and operate on yourself (well, at least you certainly shouldn't!).
This is the same with a bankruptcy. It may look straightforward to
the outsider looking in, but I can assure you that bankruptcy is an
exceedingly nuanced area of the law, with cases changing things
every day[1].

For the vast majority of my clients, this is a one-time situation in
which they are humbled, embarrassed, and scared to be facing.
A good bankruptcy attorney can greatly reduce the stress of the
entire process, make sure everything is done right, ensure that you
get a discharge against all the debts that are dischargeable, and in
general, guide you through a difficult situation no one ever plans on
being in.

---

1. Just within the last few weeks of me writing this, the U.S. Supreme Court invalidated what was assumed to be the protection for inherited IRAs. That means if you filed a case and did not take this into account, you could lose the ENTIRE IRA even though you heard retirement accounts are protected in bankruptcy.

One of the great things about my job is to be able to watch the change in my clients as I discuss how things may work in their case. Most of my clients have been in this financial situation for YEARS. It's not as though a late bill came yesterday and they don't know how to pay it. When I first talk to clients, I've seen couples break down in tears because of the stress of the situation, and I've seen the same couples leave my office after our free consultation with a kick in their step that they confess they haven't had for years. These are gratifying moments for both my clients and for me.

Alexzander C. J. Adams, Esq.

3. Will You Lose Your Home or Other Stuff in Bankruptcy?

This is typically not the case. Let's talk about how a large secured asset like a home with a mortgage works in bankruptcy. There are exemptions to property in bankruptcy. This means that you get to keep certain property worth a certain amount in certain property categories. Bankruptcy isn't like the old "Tom and Jerry" cartoon where a truck pulls up to a home to clear out all your belongings to be auctioned, and to underscore another common misconception, it is virtually impossible to get locked-up for non-payments of debts[2].

In reality, our society wants you to have certain things regardless of whom you owe money to. For instance, courts do not want your clothes, basic household goods and furniture, food supplies, and things like that. There are also exceptions for larger items, typically cars and homes.

As is the case with all property in bankruptcy, we have to look at what it is worth and what is owed on it. This will show how much equity is in the property, and we can then see how much equity

2. With the exception of failure to pay domestic support in some jurisdictions and contempt of a court order to appear in court. These are rare, and in fact I have never had this occur in a case I have had to deal with, but there are certainly stories out there where this has occurred.

we can protect. For instance, in Oregon, a married couple can typically keep $45,000–$50,000 of equity in a home they live in. So if you owe $300,000 on a house that is worth $325,000, that couple will keep the home because there is $25,000 of equity, and the bankruptcy can protect $45,000–$50,000 of equity. Homes that are underwater or worth less than what is owed on them typically are ignored by the trustee in this case because even if they sold the house, there would be no money for the trustee to collect.

So what happens when there is a lot of equity in a home? More equity than can be protected? Well, the clients have a choice if they want to file bankruptcy. If they give up the house, the trustee would sell the house and give them a check once the home is sold. For instance, let's say the above house is worth $385,000. The court would sell the house, pay the $300,000 mortgage, pay the bankruptcy filers $45,000–$50,000 for the exemptions, and then use the balance to pay a portion of the debts and trustee commissions. The exemption remains the same but has to be accounted for differently. Of course, this doesn't take into account cost of sales or marketing, sales commissions, closing costs, etc., but I think the above example provides a good idea of how it works.

What if you do not want to give up the house? Well, that is what Chapter 13 is for. In Chapter 13, over a period of up to 60 months, you would have to pay in some money toward the $40,000. The amount paid may end up being less than $40,000 overall, but there would have to be some agreement between you and the Chapter 13 trustee. The advantage in this scenario is that in Chapter 13 even when you have equity in the home beyond the exemption you are not at risk of losing the home.

Homes can be abandoned in bankruptcy as well. This essentially means that you walk away from the home during bankruptcy with no expectation to pay the mortgage or retain the home. This is an interesting position.

In some circumstances, debtors are able to live rent or mortgage payment free for YEARS.

Sometimes banks will modify a mortgage to keep you in the home or lower payments or adjust the loan terms to make it worthwhile to keep the home.

Other times, the trustee, trustee agents, debtors, or even an outside investor will short sale or litigate against the mortgage. Sometimes my clients get money for participating in this. It's quite something to walk away from a home and have the bank pay you money to move. This really happens in some cases.

However, in all cases, when abandoning a home, two things are important to remember. First, homeowners and condo association fees are due from the day of filing bankruptcy until the date of foreclosure transfer. So the mortgage goes away, but HOA and condo fees after filing continue to be assessed. Further, I recommend clients maintain a liability insurance policy on the property. This would protect a client from lawsuits for personal injury on the property from the filing of the bankruptcy until foreclosure.

In any event, losing a house is a rare circumstance in a bankruptcy, and my clients always know going in what is likely to occur.

4. Does Bankruptcy Stop a Garnishment or a Lawsuit Against My Pay?

The reason people file bankruptcy is to stop collections and wipe their slate clean of debt and claims to the extent possible, but there seems to be a lot of confusion regarding how it works. I want to talk a little about how it works and then address the specifics of this question.

Whenever a bankruptcy is filed, an order is entered into the court's docket called a "stay." A stay is a temporary cease and desist order against all[3] collections against the filer. It is designed to stop collections in their tracks, and provide a cooling-off period prior to the bankruptcy meeting of the creditors. At the conclusion of the case, typically 90 days or so in Chapter 7 and 36–60 months in Chapter 13—a discharge order is entered into the docket. A discharge order is a permanent court order ordering all the debts that can be eliminated during the bankruptcy are eliminated.

Getting the discharge order is typically the main goal of every bankruptcy. It is that order that will prevent collections against you forever for the debts that can be discharged in bankruptcy. Let me say that again—FOREVER. This means that if you owe $10,000

3.There are a few exceptions, most notably ongoing spousal and child support.

on a credit card and you received a discharge order on this debt, the credit card company can NEVER collect, sue, contact, call, or garnish you for that debt. EVER! If they do, in many circumstances you can actually sue the creditor for violating the discharge injunction. It is that powerful.

So in regards to garnishments and lawsuits[4], a bankruptcy will stop those in their tracks. Garnishments will stop after the filing of a bankruptcy, and most lawsuits will be dismissed upon the completion of the bankruptcy. Many, many people file bankruptcy to stop garnishments.

Lawsuits against you are also typically dismissed immediately or put on hold until after the bankruptcy. For instance, a collection lawsuit for a debt is typically dismissed when bankruptcy is filed, and if not dismissed immediately, it is put on hold until the discharge order is entered, and then it is dismissed. The result is the same—no collections at all after filing and a permanent bar on collections when the discharge is entered. Other lawsuits, such as divorces and foreclosure, are held until after the bankruptcy or at least until a period of time after the bankruptcy stay is in effect. Specifically with a foreclosure, it will resume after a bankruptcy (unless other arrangements are made), but there will be no entry of judgment for money[5]—the lawsuit goes on against the property but you are not liable for any money. It seems a little peculiar—suing a house or piece of land—but this makes sense to some extent, because if you could eliminate the financial liability with a mortgage but at the same time retain the property, people would get a "free house." I would think a lot of people would file bankruptcy to "get a free house," but that is not how it works. The "free house" thinking is one of the things the Internet is so fond of advocating, but it is not reality.

In the state of Oregon, the garnishment laws allow for up to 25% of after tax paycheck money to be garnished for debt. If you have

4. As there always is in the law, there are some exceptions to this, but a detailed examination of all exceptions is beyond the scope of this book. Schedule a time to go over your situation, and we can review your case in detail.
5. ...that remains unsatisfied. There is a peculiar way this works in Oregon, but there is no debt against the bankruptcy filer.

a household that relies on $4,000 a month to make ends meet, and suddenly that is reduced to $3,000, it won't take long for household finances to fall apart. Upon the filing of a bankruptcy, the stay goes into effect and the garnishments will stop.

In Oregon and other states that have generous exemptions (typically any state that uses the federal exemption scheme or has a generous wild card exemption), 90 days worth of the pre-petition garnishment can often be recovered. So, to put that in perspective, if you have been garnished $1,000 per month for the 3 months before filing, we can typically retrieve $3,000 for you, less recovery costs.

So it is not entirely uncommon to file a bankruptcy and a month or so later get a check. This doesn't happen in all cases, but it can and does happen. I really enjoy giving that check back to clients. It seems counter intuitive that in a bankruptcy you will actually get money back, but it happens sometimes!

Alexzander C. J. Adams, Esq.

5. What About My Retirement Account?

I think this is a critical consideration when filing bankruptcy. First, let's talk about what a retirement account is. For bankruptcy, we are talking about "ERISA" qualified retirement plans—401(k)s, 403(b)s, individual retirement accounts, Roth individual retirement accounts, PERS, Calpers, Thrift Saving Plans, retirement annuities—essentially the types of accounts that allow you to put in pretax earnings and you pay a penalty if you withdraw before retirement age. Often times there will be an employer match to your contributions. Retirement accounts are accounts that when you retire you plan to draw against. So for a lot of people when they hit their mid-60s, retirement includes income from three typical sources—Social Security, retirement accounts like above, and some type of employment income, either full-time or part-time.

In bankruptcy, Social Security is completely protected from collection in bankruptcy. In fact, Social Security is such an important consideration that the bankruptcy code essentially doesn't even consider Social Security income for means test purposes.

Your retirement accounts in Oregon are safe, as well[6]. Whether

6. With one significant exception. A recent US Supreme Court case held that inherited retirement accounts are not considered retirement accounts for purposes of Federal Bankruptcy Exemptions. This means if Mom or Dad pass away and give you their 401(k) account in a will, and you roll it over into a retirement account of your own of some kind, it is not protected. This could be a substantial issue in your case depending on the value of the account. Note: IF YOU HAVE THIS TYPE OF ACCOUNT—BRING IT TO YOUR ATTORNEY'S ATTENTION AT THE FIRST INTERVIEW YOU HAVE WITH THEM. Unclear is whether Oregon's or other state's exemptions protect this kind of account. This will be something to watch.

using the Federal exemptions or the Oregon exemptions, the bankruptcy rules want you to retain you retirement account. If I had a magic wand and could make everyone who is considering cashing out their retirement account to pay off debt talk to a bankruptcy attorney before doing so, I would. So please, as part of any debt payment considerations

BEFORE YOU CASH OUT A RETIREMENT ACCOUNT TO PAY DEBTS, CONSULT WITH A BANKRUPTCY ATTORNEY WHETHER YOU CHOSE TO FILE BANKRUPTCY OR NOT.

Why do I say this? Well, here's what happens.

Let's say a married couple has $50,000 of credit card debt and medical bills and $100,000 in a 401(k). They want to pay the credit cards off with the retirement account rather than consider bankruptcy. So they cash out their 401(k) of $100,000 and net approximately $60,000 from the early withdrawal after taxes. This leaves the credit cards paid off, $10,000 in their pockets that they spend, and there is no 401(k) left.

So this couple is out of debt. Well, how much did it cost them? First, it costs $50,000 to pay the debt. Then it costs $40,000 in tax payments and penalties to cash out the account. That's $90,000 to pay a $50,000 debt. So right out of the gate you are paying close to double the debt to pay it off.

Some say this is expensive, yes, but they have no debt and they have avoided bankruptcy. This is true, but this strategy also costs the lost investment income. If you can invest 6% annually for 15 years, that's another $150,000. So 15 years down the road what should have been a $250,000 nest egg to live on is gone to pay credit cards and unsecured debt.

I can't underscore this enough:

THIS CAN COST $250,000—A QUARTER OF A MILLION DOLLARS—TO PAY THIS DEBT!

Now, let's consider a typical bankruptcy option. Perhaps you have $5,000 of assets that no matter what we do, we can't protect in bankruptcy, meaning that to get the permanent protection of the bankruptcy court discharge, you will have to pay the court $5,000. You file bankruptcy, perhaps take a 401k LOAN to pay the bankruptcy trustee the $5,000 in Chapter 7 or pay the $5,000 in over 3–5 years in Chapter 13.

What's the result? You are free from the credit card bill and medical debts AND you get to your retirement account. This may seem counter intuitive, but why does it work this way? Or more importantly, why does the government let it work this way? Well, it's pretty simple.

THE GOVERNMENT AND SOCIETY WANTS YOU TO KEEP YOUR RETIREMENT.

Why you ask? Because if you don't have money to live on during retirement, you will have to rely on friends, family, and the government to make up the difference. Let's be real—it is very difficult to live on Social Security income alone. Life is just too expensive for the most part. But if you have Social Security, a retirement income you draw from (or a pension), and maybe job or hobby job income, suddenly there is the ability to survive and thrive through a modest retirement.

Remember, the purpose of the bankruptcy code is for the person or couple filing bankruptcy to get a fresh start. Part of that fresh start is to have enough income to take care of yourself. This means that in all but the rarest of situations, if you file a bankruptcy, your retirement will be protected from your creditors.

6. Will I Ever Be Able to Get Credit Again?

There is a dirty little secret that my bankruptcy clients often find out—within days of filing a bankruptcy, you will be the proud owner of a mailbox full of credit card applications and car loan solicitations. Not one or two, but many! But you say

HOW CAN THAT BE? I AM BANKRUPT!

Bankruptcy generally means your debts outweigh your ability to repay them. On the eve of filing bankruptcy, this is true. You are inundated with debt that you can't pay. There is a heavy burden on your shoulders that often builds up over many years of inability to pay debts. But a magical thing happens the very minute you file bankruptcy—you are granted a temporary court order that relieves the debt and if you follow through, this debt relief is permanent! So from a practical aspect—and certainly with only rare exception in Chapter 7—after your case is filed, it is a virtual certainty that all of the debts that can be relieved forever will be relieved forever.

What does this mean to lenders? Well, the day after bankruptcy is filed, you do not have the burden of all that debt hanging from your shoulders. So what happens?

LENDERS OFFER TO LEND YOU MONEY BECAUSE THEY KNOW YOU HAVE LITTLE DEBT, AND THE

DEBT THAT YOU DO HAVE IS DISCLOSED IN THE BANKRUPTCY PAPERWORK.

So now that you've filed and have no debt, you are once again a decent credit risk. After all, if you don't have to pay all of the other debt that will be discharged, you should have plenty of money to pay the creditors with.

If you don't think this is sleazy enough (and it is, but it gets worse)—once you complete a Chapter 7 bankruptcy and receive a discharge, **YOU CANNOT FILE BANKRUPTCY AGAIN FOR 8 YEARS** with certain exceptions. This means that if you are unfortunate enough to take on new debt and fall behind again, they have 8 years to collect, harass, garnish, and sue you! It's really an insane process, but that's how it works.

So to answer the question—clients will absolutely have access to credit after filing bankruptcy. It typically takes 2–4 years after a bankruptcy to qualify for a home loan (and in certain situations even less), but credit cards and car loans can be accessed almost immediately.

Will you pay super low interest with a large credit limit? No. Although the terms that you qualify for closer to the bankruptcy will be less than ideal, the further away you are from a bankruptcy, the better your terms will become over time. I have a number of clients who just a year or 2 after bankruptcy have no debt, very moderate 'emergency' credit lines that are paid monthly, and a credit score that typically is much higher than their score prior to filing.

Do I recommend obtaining these lines of credit? NO! One of the goals I have for my clients is to wean themselves from credit. Think about it. If a client comes in paying (or trying to pay) $1,000 per month in credit card bills, and we eliminate that debt, where does the $1,000 a month go?

The frugal debtor will pay cash for everything (or most things anyway) and put some of their money away in an account. Imagine after 12 months of putting $1,000 a month in a savings account, if you actually have a need for credit

YOU CAN BORROW IT FROM YOURSELF AND PAY YOURSELF BACK.

That is essentially a free loan with no interest, no issues if your repayment terms are late, and no tax issues if you don't pay the loan back. This is a much better way to do things, and it is certainly what I wish for my clients.

Now on a practical level, if your kid needs braces or your engine blows up and you haven't had the time to save the $12,000, then you will need access to credit to solve these problems. There will be access to credit.

One other thing I'd like to point out is if you have to travel for work or other reasons, you may think that you need a credit card to rent hotels, cars, airplanes tickets, etc. Well, the truth is you don't need the credit card, you need access to the Visa and MasterCard networks. And guess what? I'd bet dollars to donuts if you pull out your wallet or purse right now and look at your checking debit card, there is a Visa or MasterCard symbol on it. These function the same as a credit card, but they are attached to your bank account, not a credit line. A simple debit card is all that's needed for travel. Of course, you have to put some money into the checking or savings account, but the idea is when you have wiped out your debt in bankruptcy, you will be able to do that MUCH more effectively than if you had not relieved all that debt.

To reiterate something I said earlier,

BANKRUPTCY IS A BUMP IN THE ROAD, IT'S NOT THE END OF THE ROAD.

If you need credit, it will be there as time passes after the bankruptcy. But bankruptcy is a time to fundamentally change how you treat money and credit and how money and credit treat you.

TAKE THIS OPPORTUNITY TO TELL MONEY WHAT TO DO AND WHERE TO GO, RATHER THAN ALLOWING IT TO TELL YOU WHERE TO GO AND WHAT TO DO WITH IT!

7. Why Do People End Up Filing Bankruptcy?

The decision to file bankruptcy is one of the most difficult decisions a person can ever make.

Bankruptcies are filed for a lot of reasons. Here are just some examples of situations I see all the time:

1. A parent takes an awkward step during a kid's sporting activity, breaking an ankle. The ankle treatment is not covered by insurance, but the resulting injury eventually heals and things are back to normal. That is normal except for the $15,000 in medical bills from the hospital, the ambulance, the ER, the treating doctors (and maybe even the anesthesiologist and various other medical personnel).

2. A seasonal layoff puts one parent on unemployment. Already living from paycheck to paycheck just to keep food on the table for their kids and themselves, they go into debt to make up the difference. One working spouse is now back to work full time, but overtime has been cut and there doesn't seem like a realistic way to ever pay off the debts.

3. A wife is blindsided by divorce papers. After spending a year fighting for custody, visitation, and spousal support, the divorce is now over and the wife has both significant debt of her own and significant debt assigned to her through the

divorce decree, and she has no way to make ends meet in her now single-income household.

All three of these examples, and many more, are driving factors when people are considering bankruptcy. These types of bills seem to have a way of sneaking up on people when they least expect them. If you add to this threats of garnishment of paychecks or bank account levees to pay the debts, life can get very scary, very quickly for someone facing one of these types of situations.

Often when people reach my offices, we are able to trace their trouble to a specific event, which I call "the point of no return." This is the moment where the decisions of the past are turned on their head due to a change in life circumstances, and from that point on, there can be little choice regarding financial recovery without something like a bankruptcy to reset the switch and get things back on track. In the first example above, it was the broken ankle. In the second example, maybe an unusually cold winter or hot summer was the culprit. In the third, maybe it was the ex- spouse's new love interest. Whatever caused the situation really doesn't matter (in the eyes of debt collectors, anyway). In the long run, what really matters is how to dig out and get back on track.

The good news is that for the most part, bankruptcy can help resolve these debts and many others very quickly and usually for a minimal amount of money and effort compared to resolving the debts outside of bankruptcy. For instance, medical bills, past due utility bills, car repossession balances, credit card bills, and many other debts are eliminated in bankruptcy. Certain marital debt obligations can also be disposed of in Chapter 13 bankruptcies. Even certain debts that you might not expect to be resolved in a bankruptcy—such as taxes or second mortgage obligations—can be either eliminated or paid through a bankruptcy, if the facts are in line.

Each bankruptcy is unique to the individual client's situation, but the goal is always the same—to get a fresh start and to get on with life in the most efficient and economical way possible.

8. What is the Difference Between Chapter 7 Bankruptcy and Chapter 13 Bankruptcy?

Bankruptcy is designed to get everyone who files a bankruptcy a fresh financial start, free from the strappings of debt and financial oppression. While not all debts are able to be relieved in bankruptcy, most are[7].

In general, the way a bankruptcy court deals with debts and assets is the same for both kinds of cases. You must provide to the court details of all of your debts, assets, household income, size, and budget along with a statement of financial affairs that goes over some historical financial information, and a means test that ensures you are not making too much money to qualify for bankruptcy relief under Chapter 7. If you do not pass the means test, you are limited to a Chapter 13 bankruptcy with 36–60 months of monthly payments to the bankruptcy trustee, unless your debts in certain categories are too high8. Your assets are then totaled and valued and compared to your debts. If you have so many assets that the bankruptcy code cannot protect them, then you either give up the assets in Chapter 7 or pay for this difference in Chapter 13. At the end of either case, your debts

7. For instance, spousal and child support, debts obtained fraudulently, property damaged from when a debtor is intoxicated, recent taxes, restitution, and student loans are not forgiven in bankruptcy, though most every other kind of debt is. There are always exceptions to this statement. Please speak with an experienced bankruptcy lawyer regarding the debts you have and whether there are any issues with discharging them in bankruptcy. This book is not designed as a guide to file bankruptcy without a lawyer's assistance.
8. In that case you are limited to Chapter 11 bankruptcy, which is both rare and beyond the scope of this book.

are "discharged," meaning a court order is entered in your case ordering the debts be eliminated forever.

There are two credit counseling courses that you must take to get the bankruptcy discharge. One is a prefiling credit counseling course that lasts about an hour. This course is typically referred to as the "ticket in to bankruptcy relief." The second course is a two-hour financial management course that must be taken after filing but before the closing of your case. This second course is typically called the "ticket out of bankruptcy." Both courses are available online or over the phone.

So the basic end result of both Chapter 7 and Chapter 13 bankruptcies is the same—most debts are gone forever—but both chapters do the work a little bit differently.

I'll touch briefly on both chapters here, but the important thing to remember is that every individual bankruptcy case is very fact specific. The law is the same for everyone, but may work differently to people with different assets, income, and financial history.

So let's first discuss Chapter 7 bankruptcy.

Chapter 7 bankruptcy is what is generally called a liquidation bankruptcy, although most clients do not lose assets. If you are under a certain income, you can file for Chapter 7 bankruptcy, which typically involves a swift 90- to 120-day court proceeding. On the day the case is filed, a temporary court order called a "stay order" stopping all collections is entered by the court. This stops garnishments, collection calls, lawsuits, and other collection activities immediately. At the end of the case, this temporary stop order becomes permanent in the form of a "discharge" injunction order, stopping collections on the discharged debts FOREVER. The main purpose of any consumer bankruptcy is to get this order.

After filing a Chapter 7 bankruptcy, there is typically one hearing that you must attend. The meeting is called a meeting of creditors, where anyone you owe money to can ask you questions about the debt. Although anyone is allowed to ask questions at this hearing, creditors rarely show up to question debtors. Creditors in Oregon that do show up are typically ex-business partners, ex-spouses, and the tire company Les Schwab. Taxing authorities also attend occasionally depending on the seriousness of the tax debts that may be owed.

Certain debts are not relieved in Chapter 7 that may be relieved in Chapter 13. These include martial debts and moving violation fines. Other debts are paid off in Chapter 13 that would remain after the Chapter 7 discharge. These include car payments, spousal support arrears payments, and taxes. If it is found that you have assets that you must turnover to the court, you must cooperate with the court's appointed agent, who is called a trustee, so these items can be collected. About 90 days after the case is filed, the discharge order will be entered. If you are required to pay in money or contribute assets, the case will remain open after discharge to deal with the administration of the assets. Once administered, the case will then close.

Now let's take a look at Chapter 13 bankruptcy.

Chapter 13 reaches the same result as Chapter 7, but through a different process. In Chapter 13, either because you want to or because you have to, you will make a payment to the court each month for 36–60 months. This monthly payment will pay certain debts that must be paid, such as attorney fees, court trustee fees, best interest amount, car loans, priority taxes, and domestic support arrears, to name a few. So let's say a $400 monthly payment will satisfy all of these debts. After 36–60 months of payments, you receive the bankruptcy discharge, the debts that you must pay will be paid off, and the rest of the debt is discharged just like a Chapter 7 case. Generally, you are not required to pay 100% of your debt in Chapter 13, except in very rare circumstances.

There are many compelling reasons to consider Chapter 13 even if you could file a Chapter 7 bankruptcy. Among the most common reasons people cite when choosing Chapter 13 over Chapter 7 are:

- Lower payments than outside of bankruptcy;
- Shorter payments (5 years maximum compared to 25–30 years of minimum credit card payments);
- Reinstatement of driving license for violations (not crimes);
- Ability to stop garnishments and pay tax debt on their own schedule, at 0% interest with no ongoing penalties accruing;
- Ability to adjust the value of secured assets;
- Ability to eliminate secured liens against real property in some circumstances;
- Ability to stop student loan payments for up to 5 years; and
- Personal desire to pay something toward their debts.

It is not uncommon to have a client who was paying $2,000 or sometimes even more per month for what seems like the foreseeable future, to be able to pay something closer to $400 per month for 60 months and have all of their debt resolved. This can be a HUGE savings.

I generally go over both Chapter 7 and Chapter 13 options when I meet with clients. I have had many clients enthusiastic about Chapter 13 when it is explained in light of the facts in their case. I am always surprised to hear that for many of the clients who have met with other attorneys, Chapter 13 was not discussed. On the other hand, I've also seen many clients who with some planning and patience could pass the Chapter 7 means test but have been told by other attorneys that Chapter 13 is the best option for them, when the reality is Chapter 7 would be a better option.

So to recap—the results are the same, but the process is different between the two consumer chapters of the bankruptcy code, and which is the better one for a particular client must be determined by the facts and goals of that client.

That is another reason why I like my job so much. Each and every case is different, and I get to spend my time meeting and helping people from all different backgrounds and goals get out of debt.

9. Do You Have to Pay Back All of Your Debt in Chapter 13 Bankruptcy?

Chapter 13 is a method to reorganize your debts. It consists of making a monthly payment for typically 3–5 years to the bankruptcy court trustee. In exchange for this payment, certain debts are paid and certain debts are discharged—eliminated forever—from a client's life.

Let's first talk about two of reasons people typically file Chapter 13 bankruptcy rather than Chapter 7 liquidation bankruptcy. The first reason people file Chapter 13 is that they have to. What do I mean by this? I mean the bankruptcy code says that if you have a certain amount of income, you are ineligible for Chapter 7 and you must be in Chapter 13 bankruptcy and pay back a portion of your debt. This is initially verified through a "means test" to ensure those people that can pay something toward their debts do. If you do not pass the bankruptcy means test, you will be required to reorganize under Chapter 13 rather than Chapter 7. So instead of walking away from your debt, you will be required to pay a portion of it.

The second reason people file Chapter 13 is because they want to. Why would anybody want to file Chapter 13 if they could file a Chapter 7 and walk away from their debts? There are many reasons. Perhaps if they filed a Chapter 7, they may be subjected to losing some assets that they can keep in a Chapter 13 case. Maybe there are outstanding taxes or domestic support obligations that can be paid in Chapter 13 but would not be resolved in Chapter 7. Maybe there are secured debts that can get better payment terms in a Chapter 13. Maybe there are outstanding student loan issues that at this point make paying them in full unrealistic.

If you notice, none of those reasons require a 100% payback. I am often asked, "How much debt am I required to pay back in Chapter 13?" This is something I hear so much incorrect information about from the people I meet with. Typically, the debts that must be paid back are paid. If there is a minimal required payment amount to unsecured creditors, that will be paid back, and the rest of the debts are discharged.

Here is a typical example of a Chapter 13 case:

- Married couple with minor children;
- Car loan with total balance of $20,000 with 19% interest and $600 monthly car payment; car was bought 3 years ago and has a fair market value of $10,000;
- Second mortgage of $75,000, but the value of the home is significantly less than the first mortgage. Payment is $675 per month, interest only;
- $60,000 of credit card debts and medical bills. Minimum payments are $1,100 per month;
- Couple's gross income is high, but take-home pay leaves little left at the end of the month, especially after the bills are paid; and
- They haven't missed a payment yet, but they will in the next few months.

This client is ripe for assistance under Chapter 13. Without going into too much detail, this type of client can typically expect the following result:

- The payment of $600 monthly for the car, $675 monthly for the second mortgage, and $1,100 for the other bills should stop; that's $2,375 per month back in the client's pockets;

- The second mortgage would be eliminated (called "lien stripping"), and no further obligation[9] will be required on that mortgage;
- The credit cards bills will be eliminated completely;
- The car will be adjusted to a balance of $10,000 with a reduced interest rate, typically 4–5%; and
- The debtor will potentially have an initial minimum 60-month payment of something like $300 per month. This is significantly better than $2,375!

In the above example, $10,000 of the car loan is eliminated, $75,000 of the second mortgage is eliminated, and $60,000 of the unsecured medical and credit cards bills is eliminated. That's $145,000 of debt eliminated!

In this example, it is likely we can craft a budget in bankruptcy leaving little if anything to pay toward the $145,000. This would mean at the end of the above bankruptcy case, there would be a discharge of the $145,000 of debt. No taxable income, no collections, no calls, no garnishments, no debts!

Let's say the couple's gross income is very high. A family that could afford to pay something toward that $145,000 of debt will do so in Chapter 13. For instance, let's say at the end of the month, there is $500 of income that is surplus. This is a real possibility when a budget is readjusted with this type of debt load. In this scenario, if it is available, the court can make you pay the $500 per month toward the debts. In a 5-year plan, that is $30,000 of payments. This is still a huge savings over the $145,000 total, and the balance is discharged at the end of the case.

So what about this 100% payback? You can imagine a case where people with very high income may be in this type of a scenario. If the couple could afford to pay all of their debts, then the court may require a 100% payment, but this is far from the norm.

---

9. So long as you make it through the reorganization plan.

Alexzander C. J. Adams, Esq.

10. Who Are You?

Debts and bankruptcy can affect people for so many reasons. Some people are certainly careless with their money. Others perhaps had no financial education, and when they suddenly had some money, they had no idea how to handle it. Still others faced untenable market conditions that they could not recover from, and some people just have had some plain old bad luck. Just look at the U.S. economy from 2008 to present! It can affect famous and very rich people. It's true! Debts and financial problems occur through all different lifestyles and incomes. Take a look at this list of people who have declared bankruptcy:

- P.T. Barnum—Entertainment Entrepreneur
- Gary Busey—Actor
- Gary Coleman—Actor
- Governor John Connally—Governor/Passenger in JFK Assassination Car
- Francis Ford Coppola—Movie Director
- Walt Disney—Theme Park and Movie Magnate
- Henry Ford—Industrialist
- William Fox—Co-founder of 20th Century Fox Film Corporation
- Ulysses S. Grant—18th US President
- Merle Haggard—Singer
- MC Hammer—Musician

- H.J. Heinz—Condiment King
- Milton Hershey—Chocolate King
- Perez Hilton—Celebrity
- Larry King—Journalist
- Jerry Lee Lewis—The Killer
- Abraham Lincoln—16th US President
- Meatloaf—Musician
- Vince Neil—Rock and Roller
- Dave Ramsey—Radio Host and Author
- Anna Nicole Smith—Actor
- Edgar Allen Poe—Author
- Lawrence Taylor—Athlete
- Mike Tyson—Athlete

I think that looking at this list (and there are a lot more famous people who have declared bankruptcy—just do an Internet search!) you can see that no one type of person is immune from bankruptcy.

But I think what is critical to know, and what I believe, is that while bankruptcy may affect you,

BANKRUPTCY DOES NOT DEFINE YOU!

Everyone above, for the most part, bounced back—some creating empires that still exist today. How many history books that praise Lincoln over and over fail to mention his bankruptcy? Well, all of the ones I had until I became a bankruptcy attorney, that's for sure. Why? Because it's a blip in a person's life or legacy, not the legacy itself.

I wonder how many people reading this knew that all the people above filed bankruptcy. I say look at this list. If filing bankruptcy is something that you need to do, there are and will be opportunities to bounce back and excel at life. No one on the list above gave up and quit trying and neither should a person in bankruptcy now. They were perhaps all humbled by the experience, but none gave up.

I considered not putting this chapter in the book, but I think it brings a little insight into what is often a very private and guarded process.

Let me say this unequivocally—bankruptcy is a **TEMPORARY SITUATION** that you can bounce back from **IF YOU ARE WILLING TO DO THE WORK**. I am not saying it is fun or easy or something that my clients brag about, but it is not the end of the road. Rather, it is a bump in the road. There are celebrities, politicians, presidents, artists, authors, clergy, doctors, and even other bankruptcy lawyers—all types of people—who have filed bankruptcy before you and who will file after you.

You are not alone in the journey through bankruptcy.

I think of particular note is Dave Ramsey, who essentially turned his bankruptcy into a business. So humbled was Ramsey by his situation that he started a business to keep people from ever having to go through bankruptcy like he did. He was a provider of the second bankruptcy education course—the course in personal financial management—that we recommended. His business is now incredibly successful. I wonder if without his personal bankruptcy, would he have landed where he did? And because of his bankruptcy, millions of people have benefited from the lessons he learned along the way. That is a great result for someone who had to file bankruptcy.

One of my favorite parts of being a bankruptcy attorney is the clients who years later contact me for whatever reason and tell me how things have progressed since I worked with them. It seems that every week I receive notes from clients telling me how things have improved since their bankruptcy. I really enjoy knowing that I've helped the families over the long term.

11. Is It True That Bankruptcy Represents a Personal or Even a Moral Failure?

This is something that I hear from many clients, and I see it all of the time. Clients come into my office after literally YEARS of financial destitution, some are virtually homeless, their paychecks are being garnished, their bank accounts have been wiped out, but they still feel that they have to pay 40%, 50%, even 60% of their money toward their debts because there is some kind of moral obligation to pay a debt you can't afford.

I am going to say this now and I hope people reading this book hear me loud and clear. That's a load of garbage! You have a LEGAL obligation to pay these debts. But a moral obligation is between you and your family, your country, and your God. It is NOT between you and a credit card company, car lender, or mortgage company. If you haven't noticed, many of these companies have no morals.

I could go on a rant here that would last for hundreds of pages about the financial problems in this country, their sources, some possible solutions—but it doesn't really matter. I am a blue collar lawyer who works for people, not CORPORATIONS, BANKS, and certainly not INSTITUTIONS, and I help people with their situations no matter what the case.

How can I demonstrate this distinction between moral and legal debt? Well, perhaps for some I cannot show this. And it isn't for me to prove, but it is for my clients to consider an alternative perspective—that's all. Why? Because a lot of people share this moral failure belief, even though they are about to file bankruptcy. And it is HARD to accept even though they must file bankruptcy. It often delays the asking for help in their personal situation. And it truly eats them up inside. Truly this perception of failed morals is often the

SINGLE HARDEST THING FOR A BANKRUPTCY CLIENT TO RECONCILE!

Why? Because contrary to the hoopla we hear in the media—

NOBODY WANTS TO FILE A BANKRUPTCY.

I have NEVER had a client say that they maxed out their credit cards because they couldn't wait to file bankruptcy. It doesn't happen. If you made it this far in the book, take a minute and consider why you are thinking about declaring bankruptcy. It's to keep a roof over your head, food on the table, and to provide for yourself and your family. I guarantee if you are considering bankruptcy, it is not because you want to get out of your responsibilities.

PEOPLE FILE BANKRUPTCY BECAUSE THEY HAVE TO, NOT BECAUSE THEY WANT TO!

So let's look at a couple of examples and see.

OUR FACTS: A predatory car lender sells to someone, with their less-than-perfect credit, a 2002 Ford Explorer for $7,500 (I am writing this in September 2014). This is already a 12-year old car. This particular car, the Ford Explorer was the #1 car traded in during the government's cash for clunkers program (the Explorer being the #1 clunker and 5 Fords being in the top 10 in trade-ins under this program). The blue book value for this car is about $1,000. The annual interest rate is 29.99%. There are 60 payments at about $250 each per month. The payments total $15,000, so if you crunch the numbers, there is about $14,000 of profit on a car that it is likely the dealer paid $1,000 for. That is a LOT of profit from someone who can't afford to pay it. WHERE ARE THE MORALS IN THAT?

Let's take it a step farther. The car breaks down, and because of their situation, they cannot afford to repair it. So they make payments of $250 a month on a broken down car that doesn't run, further driving them into debt because now they do not have the transportation they are trying to pay for. Is there a warranty from the dealer? NO! It was sold as is/no warranty. Sorry! WHERE ARE THE MORALS IN THAT?

So what happens? They can't afford the car, so they begin to skip the payments, the car is repossessed and sold at auction (sometimes back to the same dealer through a variety of methods), and the car is sold again to another challenged debtor for $15,000 or maybe now $14,000.

Of course the dealer fixes the car, but the dealer will have an on-staff mechanic so the repairs are much cheaper than you or I would pay at a shop. So now there is a deficiency balance and monthly payments that the original buyer owes of $14,000 at $250 per month, and they are without a car! And the new victim is paying the same $250 on the same car. So the dealer is collecting $500 per month, on a $1,000 car, from two different people, and only one person has the car. You get the idea. WHERE ARE THE MORALS IN THAT?

If they don't pay the $250, the first debtor will be sued and garnished. In Oregon, that can mean 25% of a take-home paycheck to be applied to a terrible loan that is still accruing 29.99% interest per year (plus now add attorney's fees and court fees). WHERE ARE THE MORALS IN THAT?

How about a credit card? Maybe in college they got a free T-shirt to sign up for a credit account. A T-SHIRT! T-shirts cost about

$1–2 per shirt to have made. They're in college and typically have no ability to pay, but the lender wants them on their books early anyway. After all, brand loyalty is critical to establish early on in a future debtor's life. Of course, through high school and college, are people generally taught basic financial information on how to budget and manage money? NO. So they graduate college with a bunch of credit cards—and of course student loans—that have been racked up, because a predatory lender gave them a free t-shirt. WHERE ARE THE MORALS IN THAT?

So they get out in the real world, get a job, but between student loans and family responsibilities, they make minimum payments for years. Eventually the balance is too high to handle, and they default. Does ANYONE hold the lender responsible, perhaps even a tiny bit, that their debts are partially a result of unfettered access to credit no matter whether they could pay or not? NO! It is always their fault, and the credit card companies have no culpability. WHERE ARE THE MORALS IN THAT?

If they default on a debt, and they are doing their best to pay it but can't, why does no one say, "Well, the lender is partially to blame because their credit worthiness standards were weak, because their underwriting departments pushed through any loan to get commissions, because the person approving credit increases just didn't review things as carefully as they should, or perhaps they knew the loan would place the borrower in a lifetime of financial slavery, but they did it anyway because they are greedy money hungry profiteers trying to make a buck no matter what the consequences are it places on its clients?" NO! WHERE ARE THE MORALS IN THAT?

Does anyone hold the lenders accountable for those terrible mortgages that sunk the middle class over the last 10 years? NO. It is always blamed on the borrower, and not the lender. I say claptrap[10]. I call hogwash[11] on all of this!

---

10. I had to look it up, too, but the thesaurus feature in my word processors comes up with some humdingers sometimes! A Claptrap is absurd or nonsensical talk or ideas.
11. Nonsense.

While there is certainly some blame to be apportioned to people unable to pay their bills (and yes, there is a small portion of people who can be fully blamed for their predicament), it is SHARED BLAME. Why is this?

LENDERS DO NOT LEND TO YOU BASED ON YOUR MORALS, THEY LEND TO YOU ON YOUR ABILITY TO PAY.

SO IF A LENDER DOESN'T TREAT YOU WITH THE EQUIVALENT LEVEL OF MORALS THAT YOU HAVE, YOU SHOULD NOT WORRY TOO MUCH ABOUT TREATING THEM WITH YOUR HIGH STANDARDS OF MORALS WHEN YOU ARE FILING BANKRUPTCY TO PROTECT YOURSELF AND YOUR FAMILY.

BANKRUPTCY IS A BUSINESS DECISION ABOUT YOUR PERSONAL BUSINESS—YOURSELF, YOUR FAMILY, AND YOUR HOME—AND NOTHING MORE.

DON'T LET A FALSE MORALITY ARGUMENT FROM AN INDUSTRY WITHOUT MORALS AFFECT YOUR ABILITY TO GET HELP FROM THE BANKRUPTCY COURT IF YOU NEED IT.

The truth of the matter is that it is <u>both</u> the borrower's and the lender's fault that the loans are in default. Perhaps the borrower shouldn't have borrowed, but perhaps the lender shouldn't have lent, as well.

I challenge my clients from time to time to ask their credit card companies to work with them to craft new temporary payments that are affordable. This never occurs. If they aren't willing to help, I then suggest talking to a manager about why the bank shouldn't have lent them the money in the first place. If you want to hear the sound of silence on the other end of the phone, or perhaps some snickering or giggling, call a lender and suggest that they are responsible for the defaulted debt because they shouldn't have lent to you and that they are partially to blame. Further offer to split the blame with them and tell them you'll pay your 50% of the debt that is your fault if they pay the 50% that is their fault. It's almost laughable to hear the reactions, but if you spend some time and think about it, in many situations, the above is true.

Let's take the case of a Single Guy against Big Bank. Big Bank (a person in the eyes of the law under Citizen United, 558 U.S. 310 (2010)) blames Single Guy (literally a single guy) for defaulting on a debt. When Single Guy blames Big Bank, he never talks to "the bank"—he talks to a representative of the bank, or an employee, or a division of the bank. Why? Because

THERE IS NO PERSON CALLED THE BANK!

It is a corporation. And corporations are groups of shareholders ordering the board, chairman, and corporate workers around to "maximize shareholder value". The people you talk to are not personally liable. So I say a collection of people who have no individual responsibility

CAN HAVE NO MORALS.

Lastly, and this may be a little unusual to think about, we all pay interest on debt. Some people pay more than others, but we all pay. Interest rates represent the riskiness of the loan—the higher the interest, the more risky the loan. Banks, although not moral, are not stupid. So when they calculate the interest rate on the debt, they include a factor that assumes a certain percentage of the debt will never be paid. Who pays this "loss premium?" WE ALL DO! What this means is that all of the interest you have paid before bankruptcy and all the interest you will pay after the bankruptcy has paid for all of the debt that is forgiven in all bankruptcies. I promise you in a big picture perspective this is accurate.

So, to say it clearly:

THE DEBTS YOU AND EVERY OTHER DEBTOR DISCHARGES IN BANKRUPTCY—THE ESSENTIAL

Alexzander C. J. Adams, Esq.

COST TO BUSINESS AND SOCIETY FOR BANKRUPTCY DEBTS—ARE ALREADY ACCOUNTED FOR IN THE SYSTEM AND PAID FOR WITH INTEREST.

This means that at least for the big lenders, they are already collecting interest to cover the debts you are discharging in bankruptcy, and they are then imposing some sort of moral duty on a debtor to pay the debts. WHERE ARE THE MORALS IN THAT? There are none.

People in bankruptcy are in bankruptcy to get a fresh start and move on with their lives. I have yet to have a bankruptcy client that wants to file bankruptcy. My clients HAVE to file bankruptcy because they have either exhausted all other options, or there are no other options. This is not a moral obligation. This is a legal obligation that is discharged in bankruptcy.

Morals are for family, friends, God, country, charity—you get the idea. Morals are not something a lender extends to a client. In fact, the law assumes that people do business 'at arm's length' to specifically eliminate all the moral arguments. It's strictly a legal business situation. So

WHY SHOULD YOU BE HELD TO A HIGHER MORAL STANDARD WHEN YOUR CREDITORS ARE HELD TO A LEGAL STANDARD?

Before I finish this, I want to point out one thing. For lenders, bankruptcy is only a BUSINESS DECISION. What happens when a business has money issues that it can't resolve? Well, they typically have a board meeting and elect to file Chapter 11 business bankruptcy. Why? Because debt and financing for business is a BUSINESS DECISION and NOT a MORAL DECISION. Why do businesses get to have business decisions and you and I have to have moral obligations? That is a double standard and a load of garbage. And it's an age-old scam to further indenture those in the worst situation to deal with it.

Whew. I guess after seeing this behavior over and over and over by these lenders and institutions I get sick of hearing the moral arguments. I see many clients beaten down over years of guilt that have affected their families and in many cases affected their health and well being. And I don't buy these arguments.

One last thing, perhaps another way to talk about morals it to say this. After bankruptcy is done, _when my clients are back on their feet_, if they want to pay all of their discharged debts back to the banks, they can. There is no prohibition against it. So if you can't overcome the moral issue, I get it. I am not trying to change your morals or discount your beliefs. But if bankruptcy is something you need to do for now, get a fresh start to your finances, and then later, when you are stable, you can pay back the debt. What's the advantage of this? Well, the lenders can't bug you about it! Their debts are eliminated in the bankruptcy, and you are protected from collection and harassment by the permanent bankruptcy injunction.

12. When Can I File the Case?

People often want to know how fast a case can be filed. The short answer is it can be filed TODAY if the client absolutely needs to and can do all of the things that need to be done. The practical answer is very quickly, within days if needed. Why would a person need to file quickly? Here are some common reasons:

1. **Pending foreclosure**: When people fall behind on their mortgage but want to keep their house, there can sometimes be an almost animalistic desire to keep their home. Often it's a family home, often kids are involved, still other times the client may realistically have no other living options at the time. As I've spoken about elsewhere in this book, the bankruptcy court's protection begins instantly the minute a case is filed. All collection activity grinds to a halt, and everything is initially handled by the bankruptcy court. This includes stopping foreclosures. There are reported cases in bankruptcy where there is a Sheriff 's sale or real estate trustee's sale scheduled at 10:00AM and a bankruptcy case protecting the property is filed at essentially 9:59AM. That 1 minute is enough to stop the foreclosure and allow the client an opportunity to attempt to cure the default.

2. **Repossession**: Just like a foreclosure, the filing of a bankruptcy case will stop a pending automobile repossession and allow the client to attempt to restructure or redeem the

loan. It can even be used in certain situations to get back a car that has been repossessed.

3. **Garnishment**: A garnishment is essentially where someone you owe money to can directly access your bank account balance to pay part of the debt or to take a percentage of your after-tax work wages to pay the debt, typically 25%.

   a. If a bank garnishment for over $600 has been taken from a client bank account just before bankruptcy, in a lot of circumstances we can get a portion or all of the garnished monies back. There are other factors, such as timing since garnishment and amount of garnishment, but a lot of the time I can file a case and recover the garnishment for my client.

   b. If a wage garnishment is pending for payday on Friday, and we can file the case on a Thursday, the garnishment will stop. There are some practical considerations meaning sometimes the garnishment will still come out of the paycheck, but it will be returned.

There are other urgent reasons to file a bankruptcy case, but these are the reasons I see over and over again.

So if for whatever reason a case has to be filed by Friday and it is Monday, there is plenty of time to get things done that need to be done to get the case filed. Typically, at a minimum, to file a case, here is what is needed:

1. Proof of ID and Social Security card;
2. List of all creditors (and at minimum, the creditor that the protection is needed from);
3. Completion of the consumer credit counseling course; and
4. Payment arrangements satisfied for both the attorney and the court filing fees.

This is enough to get what we call an emergency petition filed. We then have a couple of weeks to fill in the missing information, dot the i's and cross the t's.

More often, a bankruptcy takes a few weeks or a month to put together.

Typically, a potential client will meet with me for a free consultation. I do this with all of my clients in bankruptcy. It's not free per se, I am giving you an investment of my time to see if I want to represent them, and they are giving me some of their valuable time to see if they want to hire me, but there is no money exchanged, just time.

Once the client decides to file a bankruptcy, we'll go over the information I need and the fee structure. Once the prefiling fees are paid and they provide me with the information I need, we draft the case. This can take anywhere from a few days to a few months or even longer for some clients. Once the bankruptcy paperwork is drafted, they'll review the paperwork, sign it to ensure it's accurate, and we'll file it with the court.

The actual filing of the case is done electronically at my office. I've had some clients who get really involved in the case and actually want to push the filing button. So after the case is ready to file, we'll prepare it and actually have the client come back and push the button to file the case with the court. This can bring a little bit of levity to the situation, plus it's kind of fun for the client to actually see on the computer screen how the case is filed with the court.

Alexzander C. J. Adams, Esq.

13. Can Bankruptcy Help With Tax Debt?

Taxes drive a lot of people into bankruptcy. Commonly, there are four types of tax situations that you see in bankruptcy:

1. **Priority taxes**: meaning these debts must be paid in Chapter 13 or they are not discharged in Chapter 7;
2. **Non-priority taxes**: are dischargeable; these debts go away like credit card debt in Chapter 7 and Chapter 13;
3. **Secured tax debts of both priority and non-priority status**: these debts don't go away because they are tied to an asset (although there are ways to handle these debts); and
4. **Non-priority non-dischargeable taxes**: typically unresolvable in bankruptcy.

Priority tax debt means the taxes don't go away in bankruptcy. In Chapter 13, you pay them in full, or you do not get a discharge, and in Chapter 7, you simply get a discharge against other debts but not these debts. So in some cases, we file a bankruptcy knowing that there will be outstanding tax debt at the end of the case even though the case goes forward for reasons other than tax debt discharge.

Another common type of tax debt is non-priority dischargeable tax debt, which involves a tax that is for a tax period over 3 years ago and has some other things that apply (typically filing of the returns on time and aren't tax assessment and no fraud is involved in the return). In both Chapter 13 and Chapter 7, this type of tax debt is discharged and treated just like credit card debts or medical debts

Secured taxes are another type of tax debt. Sometimes the federal and state taxing agencies file liens against your personal and real property. If the debt is a dischargeable non-priority debt but secured, the debt goes away in bankruptcy as to you, but remains attached to the property. The practical affect is that you must still deal with the tax debt. In Chapter 7, there is essentially no release for this debt against your property, although once you submit the bankruptcy documents to the court, the taxing authority may review them and think that whatever property they could collect is not worth the hassle. In Chapter 13, you can either pay the debt in full, or, you pay the debt to the value of the property secured by the debt, and then the rest of the debt is eliminated. How does this work?

Well, let's say you have $5,000 worth of stuff, and $50,000 worth of tax liens attached to your stuff. In Chapter 13, once you pay the $5,000 to the taxing authority (and assuming the case discharges), the tax lien is satisfied. This is called a cram down. It makes sense because if the taxing authority took all your stuff to pay the taxes, they would not get the full debt paid, they would get the $5,000. So instead of giving up everything to pay Uncle Sam, you pay the value of your stuff. It can get a lot more complicated than that, but that's how it works (and it also works like this for cars in Chapter 7 through a process called redemption).

The last tax debt is non-priority tax debt that is non-dischargeable. This is typically from a situation of unfiled tax returns or failure to pay payroll trust account taxes. So let's say you didn't file taxes 6 years ago, but the IRS assessed $5,000 worth of tax liability. It's over 3 years old so it is within the type of tax debts that go away in bankruptcy, but because you didn't file the taxes at all, it is not a debt that will be eliminated.

Surprisingly, Chapter 13 bankruptcy is a way to sometimes pay your delinquent tax obligations (at 0% interest with no penalties) over 5 years while eliminating most or all of the other debt obligations you have.

Conclusion

I wrote this book to give people an idea of who I am and to give them some basic insight into how consumer bankruptcy works in Oregon. I've found that the perception of how bankruptcy works is greatly different from bankruptcy's reality. Keep in mind, all bankruptcy situations are unique based on the facts of an individual case. Nothing in this book is designed to be legal advice. Lastly, this book is not designed to be an exhaustive review of the law. Some nuances have been omitted, and certain things have been streamlined for a non-practitioners understanding of bankruptcy. But if after reading this book there sounds like some of the relief that I write about would help you, it makes sense to have an evaluation of your situation for bankruptcy.

Bankruptcy is an exhaustive topic, and there are many more things to discuss, but I think I have provided enough information so you know if this sounds like it might be an option for you. If you have questions about this book, including suggestions for my next book, do not hesitate to contact me.

I can be reached via email at book@PortlandBK.com or by phone at (844)-BK-DEBTS.

Closing Thoughts

If you are considering bankruptcy, here are some things to gather and bring to the first meeting with the attorney, as well as some things that you should not do until you speak with an attorney.

All of the things on the lists below are helpful to review when discussing bankruptcy or have caused trouble in bankruptcy cases in the past. This is not an exhaustive list, but these are some typical things I think are important to review and be aware of when meeting with an attorney.

Useful documents to bring to a first meeting:

1. Three bureau credit reports available for free at www.AnnualCreditReport.com.
2. Six months of income history—pay stubs, award letters, and profit and loss statements.
3. Any collection letters, lawsuits, judgments, or legal papers.
4. Initial estimate of the value of your real estate and vehicles. For real estate, www.zillow.com is a good start. For vehicle, www.kbb.com is a good start.
5. Two months of statements for any bank account you are on;
6. Two most recent years federal and state tax returns.
7. Information on any previous bankruptcies you filed.
8. Divorce decree if divorced in last 10 years.

9. A list of any and all questions or concerns you think of when gathering these documents.

Useful things to do and not to do prior to your first meeting with the attorney:

1. Talk to your attorney about any upcoming major financial changes.
2. Avoid credit card cash advances, convenience checks, and balance transfers.
3. Do not pay money, give gifts, or transfer property or title to property to family, friends, or anyone else without discussing with your attorney.
4. Do not file bankruptcy if you are about to receive a tax return or inheritance without discussing with your attorney.
5. Tell your attorney about your small business, sole proprietorship, partnership, LLC, LLP, corporation, or hobby interests.
6. Do not cash out retirement plans or 401k accounts, take out a second mortgage or payday loans, gamble, fail to disclose assets or debts, or write bad checks.
7. Do not incur your credit cards in advance of filing bankruptcy.
8. Do not tell anyone about your exploration of bankruptcy.

APPENDIX

Bankruptcy Violations
and how to report them to your attorney

A violation in bankruptcy occurs anytime a debt is attempted to be collected during the bankruptcy without express permission of the court to collect the debt; or, if after the bankruptcy discharge, an attempt to collect any discharged debt is made.

<u>Here is how to spot this and report it.</u>

Prior to filing:

Make sure each and every creditor is listed in your bankruptcy petition. It is YOUR RESPONSIBILITY to ensure that each and every person you owe money to or even may owe money to is listed in the bankruptcy. Your attorney will help instruct you on how to gather this information; but you as the client must make sure all creditors make it on the bankruptcy documents.

FIRST:

Write down your CASE NUMBER and DATE OF FILING HERE so you always have it handy.

CASE NUMBER: _____

DATE OF FILING: _____

Whenever you are contacted, give the offending creditor the case number and date of filing, and ask them to stop contacting you because you are in bankruptcy.

SECOND:

If you are contacted by any creditor AFTER filing—ANY attempt to collect, including phone calls, in person visits, collections letters, lawsuits, garnishments, failure to release a garnishment—notify the attorney of the contact.

For my client, contacts to you AFTER the date of filing should be reported to my office.

Report the contact to: **violation@portlandbk.com**. Use the following email format:

SUBJECT LINE: Violation - Client Name - Contacted by creditor name on date/time.

EMAIL BODY: ABC123 collections called 5 times after filing on the follow dates. They called my phone number of 555-555-1212. Attached are screenshots. I also forward copies of the voicemails. When I told the person calling they were rude, and said they didn't care about the bankruptcy and wanted money. The person who called was Mrs. Smith, agent 123455, calling for 555-111-1111.

TELL ME HOW UPSET THIS MADE YOU AND HOW MUCH TIME YOU HAD TO DEAL WITH THIS HARASSMENT IN ADS MUCH DETAIL AS POSSIBLE: I received these five phone calls on the same day. Two calls were at 5:45 AM and 5:49 AM, and later that evening I received calls at 6:00 PM, 6:14 PM, and 7:21 PM. In the evening, I was attending a family function, and I had to keep leaving to deal with the calls. I then had to spend about a half an hour typing this up and emailing you.

VERIFICATION Of BANKRUPTCY: I reviewed the signed bankruptcy petition you provided, and this creditor is lifted in the bankruptcy.

THIRD:

We'll review the claim for existing clients and past clients and be in touch. We do not pursue every claim, and every claim is not necessarily the type of claim that makes sense to pursue, however, it is worth notifying this office.

Thank you for reviewing this very important page of my book. The more involved you are in your case, the greater the bankruptcy benefit you will receive.

NOTE TO OREGON BANKRUPTCY FILERS IF I DID NOT FILE YOUR BANKRUPTCY CASE.

My office will review your potential bankruptcy violation claims if you received collections efforts after filing bankruptcy. In additional to the above information, please provide my office with:

- Your complete bankruptcy petition, all schedules, and a copy of discharge order, along with any other copies of collections efforts. In addition, call my office before you submit these documents to discuss your potential case. I do not charge for case review inquires.

Made in the USA
Columbia, SC
01 June 2018